Music Theory Foundations
Grade 5

Straight forward, step-by-step, explanations
for all Grade 5 Music Theory concepts.

Jade Bultitude

ISBN: 9798747165533

INTRODUCTION

Welcome to Music Theory Foundations. This book has been written to give you a deep understanding of Grade 5 music theory. In this book we will lay the foundations for understanding in all of the topics for Grade 5 music theory but also for your general music theory understanding.

Using this book for support alongside a teacher or workbook will ensure a secure knowledge of all topics. No more forgetting what you have been taught each week! Each topic is explained in easy, step-by-step, bitesize pieces to ensure effective learning.

This book explains each topic in depth so that when answering questions in the exam paper, you have a solid understanding of which techniques you can use and why they work. By understanding each concept from the ground up not only will you pass your exam with flying colours, but you will enjoy the subject! Music theory is an incredibly satisfying subject to take and I hope we can build your love and passion for it.

We provide all round preparation for the new syllabus and style of exam with simple language and lots of musical examples.

Free resource sheets that accompany each chapter can be downloaded from:

musictheoryfoundations.com/book/resources

Go and build your Music Theory Foundations!

PREREQUISITE KNOWLEDGE

Before beginning this book it is important to make sure that you have some prior knowledge. This book focuses on the ABRSM Grade 5 theory requirements. Included is some revision of topics such as clefs, intervals and chords. However, there are certain things you need to make sure you know before reading this book for everything to make complete sense.

- Note lengths of demisemiquaver, semiquaver, quaver, crotchet, dotted crotchet, minim, dotted minim, semibreve, breve and respective rests.

- All Simple and Compound time signatures, as well as their groupings. The meaning of duple, triple and quadruple.

- Be able to read notes in the Treble, Bass and Alto clefs, including those using ledger lines. You should also be able to move between these three clefs without changing the pitch of your notes.

- Accidentals including double sharps and flats. You should also have an understanding of enharmonic equivalent notes.

- All scales up to five sharps and flats, both major and minor keys. The difference between harmonic and melodic minor scales.

- The degrees and technical names of your notes i.e. tonic, supertonic etc.

- Intervals up to, but not exceeding, an octave including use of descriptive words such as major, minor, perfect, diminished and augmented.

- Be able to identify the triads of I, IV and V in root position, in all keys up to five sharps and flats.

RHYTHM AND TIME SIGNATURES

REGULAR TIME SIGNATURES

• The first type of time signatures we will look at are regular time signatures. A regular time signature will have two, three or four beats per bar and we refer to them as duple, triple or quadruple.

• There are two types of regular time signatures: **simple** and **compound**.

• Irregular time signatures make up the second group of time signatures but we will discuss this later on in the chapter.

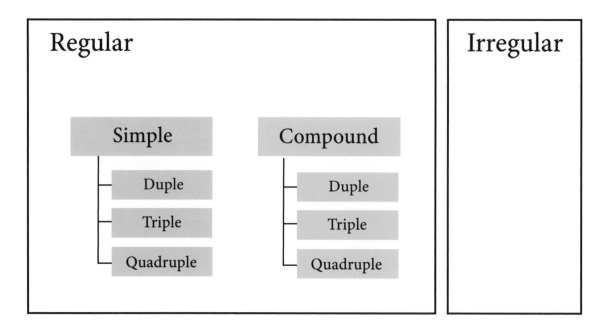

WHAT ARE SIMPLE AND COMPOUND TIME SIGNATURES?

- A **Simple** time signature has main beats that can be divided into 2.

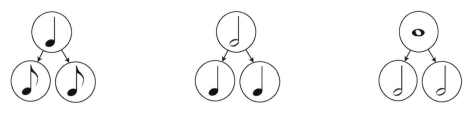

- A **Compound** time signature has main beats that can be divided into 3.

- The table below shows the most common Simple and Compound time signatures.

Simple	$\frac{2}{4}$ $\frac{2}{2}$ $\quad$ $\frac{3}{8}$ $\frac{3}{4}$ $\frac{3}{2}$ $\quad$ $\frac{4}{4}$ $\frac{4}{2}$
Compound	$\frac{6}{8}$ $\frac{6}{4}$ $\quad$ $\frac{9}{8}$ $\frac{9}{4}$ $\quad$ $\frac{12}{8}$ $\frac{12}{4}$

Regular Time Signatures

HOW CAN WE MOVE BETWEEN SIMPLE AND COMPOUND TIME SIGNATURES?

- Remember that the main beats in a Simple time signature divide into two.

- When moving between Simple time and Compound time, you will need this division of two to become a division of three. To do this you need to use a **duplet** sign.

- Alternatively, a duplet can also be written as the example below.

- The main beats in a Compound time signature divide into three.

- When moving from Compound time to Simple time, you will need these three notes to take up the space of two. To do this you need to use the **triplet** sign.

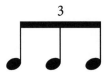

- In a Compound time signature, your main beats will require dots like this.

- Remember that by adding the dot you add half the value of the note on again. This will now mean that each beat can easily be divided into three.

• Simple time signatures do not require dots because each main beat only divides into two.

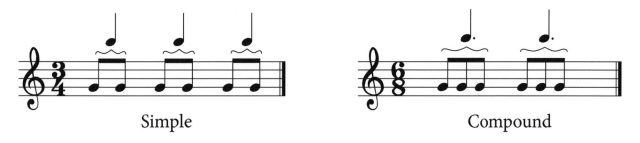

Simple   Compound

• Below are two examples of moving between Simple and Compound time signatures.

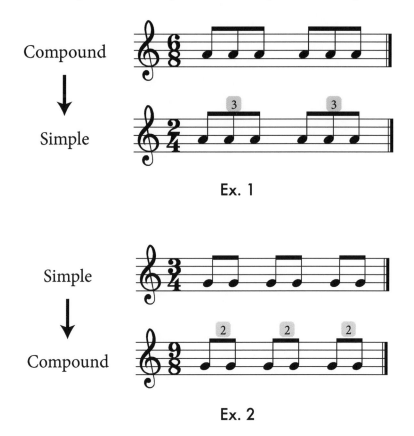

Ex. 1

Ex. 2

• Remember our Simple and Compound time signatures also fall into three different categories.

- **Duple** - meaning two main beats in a bar

- **Triple** - meaning three main beats in a bar

- **Quadruple** - meaning four main beats in a bar

Duple	$\frac{2}{4}$ $\frac{2}{2}$ $\frac{6}{8}$ $\frac{6}{4}$
Triple	$\frac{3}{8}$ $\frac{3}{4}$ $\frac{3}{2}$ $\frac{9}{8}$ $\frac{9}{4}$
Quadruple	$\frac{4}{4}$ $\frac{4}{2}$ $\frac{12}{8}$ $\frac{12}{4}$

- These labels are very useful to remember because if you start with a simple **duple** time signature you will move to a compound **duple** time signature and vice versa. This is the same for triple and quadruple time signatures.

	Simple	Compound
Duple	$\frac{2}{4}$ ⇄	$\frac{6}{8}$
Triple	$\frac{3}{4}$ ⇄	$\frac{9}{8}$
Quadruple	$\frac{4}{4}$ ⇄	$\frac{12}{8}$

- Alongside Compound and Simple time signatures we also have Irregular Time Signatures.

Key Facts

- It is important to understand what **main** beats are.

- In the time signature 4/4 there are four crotchet beats in each bar. Each of these beats is also a **main** beat because it will be counted 1…2…3…4…. This is true for all Simple time signatures.

- Compound time signatures are different. In the time signature 6/8 we have six quaver beats in a bar. However, we don't count all six quaver beats. We count in dotted crotchets, meaning it has only **two main beats**.
  ONE…two…three…**ONE**…two…three…

- It is important to know how we count the main beats in each time signature. This may seem like a trivial distinction now, but it will really help you as we move on to Irregular time signatures.

WHAT IS AN IRREGULAR TIME SIGNATURE?

- An Irregular time signature cannot fit into our three categories of duple, triple or quadruple.

- The most common Irregular time signatures that you will see are:

- An Irregular time signature's main beats do not divide up equally.

- **5/4** – 5 crotchet beats in a bar. A 5/4 bar has two main beats, but these are not equal. This can be divided in two different ways: a minim followed by a dotted minim or a dotted minim followed by a minim.

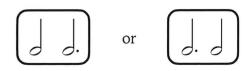

- **7/4** – 7 crotchet beats in a bar. A 7/4 bar has three main beats, but these are not equal. This can be divided in two different ways: dotted minim, minim, minim or minim, minim, dotted minim.

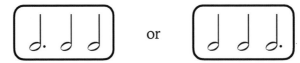

- **5/8** – 5 quaver beats in a bar. A 5/8 bar has two main beats, but these are not equal. This can be divided in two different ways: a crotchet followed by a dotted crotchet or a dotted crotchet followed by a crotchet.

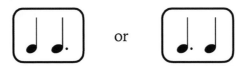

- **7/8** – 7 quaver beats in a bar. A 7/8 bar has three main beats, but these are not equal. This can be divided in two different ways: crotchet, crotchet, dotted crotchet or dotted crotchet, crotchet, crotchet.

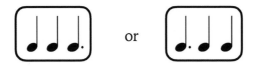

- **Remember:** In a 7/8 or 7/4 time signature, the dotted note will never be in the middle!

Key Facts

2 beats per bar = Duple Time

3 beats per bar = Triple Time

4 beats per bar = Quadruple Time

5 beats per bar = Quintuple Time

7 beats per bar = Septuple Time

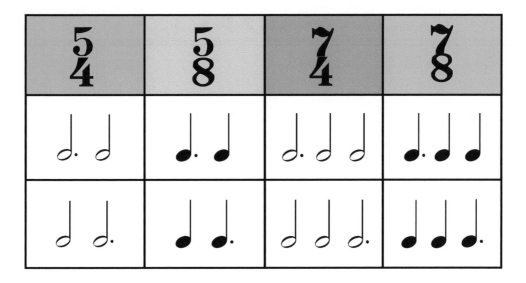

Irregular Time Signature Groupings

IRREGULAR TIME DIVISIONS

• The most common irregular time divisions that we have already seen are triplets and duplets. A **triplet** shows that you have three notes in the space of two. A **duplet** shows that you have two notes in the space of three.

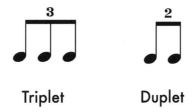

Triplet   Duplet

• For Grade 5 theory you also need to be confident with two other irregular time divisions.

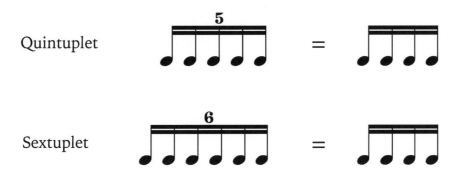

Quintuplet

Sextuplet

15

CLEFS

WHAT IS A CLEF?

- A clef is written at the start of your music. It is always written on the left hand side of the stave. It assists you in knowing what the notes are.

- The clef is used to indicate which line represents which note and this changes depending on which clef is used.

- There are four main clefs that you should be confident with for Grade 5.

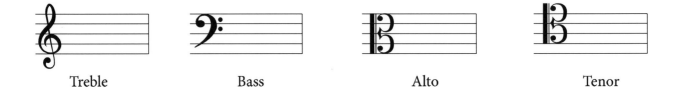

Treble   Bass   Alto   Tenor

TREBLE CLEF

- This clef is used for instruments that play notes above Middle C. For example, you would use a treble clef for the flute, clarinet, violin, and the right hand notes on the piano.

- This clef is often referred to as the G clef. This is because the start of the clef, in the middle, begins where the note G would be placed.

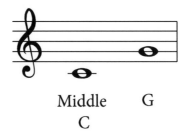

Middle   G
C

BASS CLEF

- This clef is used for instruments that play notes below Middle C. For example, you would use a bass clef for the cello, bassoon, double bass, and the left hand notes on the piano.

- This clef is often referred to as the F clef. This is because the note F is between the dots.

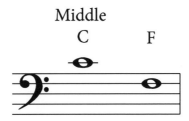

- These two clefs make up the grand stave as shown below.

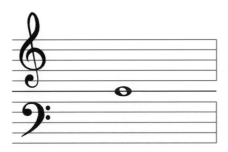

The Grand Stave

The Grand Stave

- The Grand stave is simply a treble clef stave on top and a bass clef stave on the bottom.

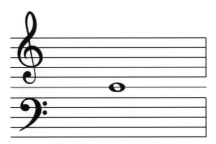

- Notice how when we draw the two staves like this, there is only **one** extra ledger line. The note on this ledger line is **always** Middle C.

- By understanding the Grand Stave, it is possible to see how to move the notes between the treble and bass clefs, when we have one without the other.

- For example, if we want to write the **B below Middle C**, this is how it would look on the Grand Stave and then in both of the clefs.

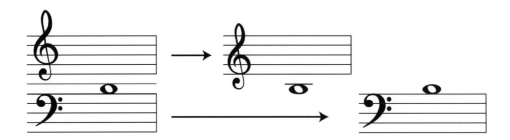

- Let's try one more, what about the **E above Middle C.**

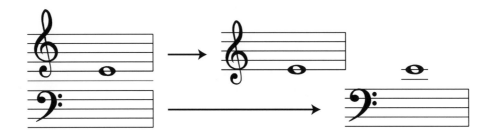

Alto and Tenor Clef

- The other two clefs you should be comfortable with are the **Alto Clef** and the **Tenor Clef**. Both of these clefs are examples of the 'C clef'. This is because Middle C appears in the middle.

Key Fact

- The Alto and Tenor Clef look the same when not on the stave. It is the positioning of this C clef on the stave that determines which clef we have.

ALTO CLEF

- The Alto Clef is most commonly used for the viola. Middle C in this clef falls on the 3rd line of the stave.

Middle C

TENOR CLEF

- The Tenor Clef is used for the upper registers of instruments that usually use the bass clef. Examples of these instruments would be the cello, bassoon and trombone.

- Middle C in this clef falls on the 4th line up on the stave.

Middle C

Here we have Middle C written in all four clefs

- Isn't it amazing how you can write the same note in these different clefs and whichever clef you use to play it in, the note will sound the same!

TRANSCRIBING BETWEEN CLEFS

- Sometimes we may be asked to transcribe between the clefs. As we have seen, this is very easy to do between treble and bass clef. Particularly if you are comfortable with the Grand Stave.

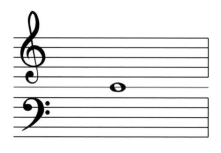

The Grand Stave

- If either the treble or bass section of the grand stave is taken away, we can replace this with ledger lines. But no matter what, we always use Middle C as a reference point.

- This is also the same when we want to transcribe into the Alto and Tenor Clefs. Use Middle C as a reference point.

- Remember, both the Alto and Tenor Clefs are what we call 'C' clefs. This means in the middle of the clef is the note Middle C. By using this as a reference point you can easily move between them.

Examples

- Here we have the E just above Middle C, transposed from the Treble Clef to the Alto Clef.

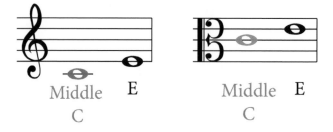

- Here we have the F just below Middle C, transposed from the Bass clef to the Tenor clef.

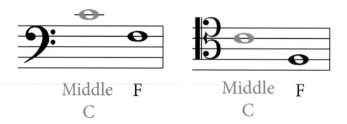

- Always use Middle C as a reference point and don't be scared of those ledger lines.

HOW TO WRITE KEY SIGNATURES IN EACH CLEF

- Once you are happy with all four clefs it is important to know how to write your key signatures. Having a key signature at the start of the piece is an essential component of music, as it informs the performer which key (scale) they will be playing in.

- As a general rule, the first sharp of the key signature will be high up on the stave, with the next one going down, then back up etc.

A Major

- As a general rule, the first flat of the key signature will be lower on the stave, with the next one going up, then back down etc.

Eb Major

- There is a very specific order in which the sharps and flats are written and it is important for you to remember this as the order **never** changes.

- Here is a handy mnemonic to help you remember.

- This is a very useful rhyme that makes it much easier to remember which order the sharps and flats need to go in.

- The first sharp scale is G major. This scale has **one** sharp. This sharp **must** be F sharp because the order of sharps never changes.

- The next sharp scale is D major. This scale has **two** sharps. These sharps **must** be F sharp and C sharp because the order of sharps never changes. See how the rhyme helps us to remember the order.

- This rule also applies to the flat scales. The first flat scale is F major. This scale has **one** flat. This flat **must** be B flat because the order of flats never changes. The next flat scale is B flat major. This scale has **two** flats. These flats **must** be B flat and E flat because the order of flats never changes.

- Below we have the key signatures of B major and D flat major. Both of these scales contain 5 sharps or 5 flats.

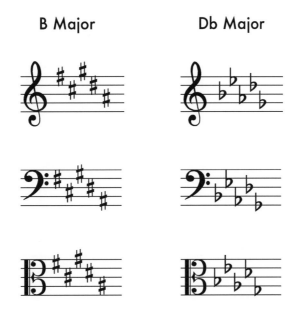

- As you can see the first sharp is always high up on the stave, the second one is lower, the third one is higher and we continue in this pattern going up and down, until we get to A sharp **where we go down again.**

- The flats begin low on the stave, go up and then down and continue in this way.

Tenor clef is a little different

- The key signature of flats follows the same rule as the other clefs. We start on the B low down on the stave and then move up to the E, down to the A and so on and so forth.

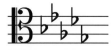

This is the tricky bit

- The key signature of sharps, rather than starting high up on the stave like all the other clefs, starts at the bottom of the stave.

Key Fact

- All key signatures follow the same rule **except** Tenor Clef sharp key signatures.

SCALES AND KEY SIGNATURES

- Scales and key signatures are very important, not only for your music theory knowledge but also if you want to play any piece of music or even compose.

- For Grade 5 you must be confident with **all** of your scales up to **six** sharps and flats.

- Before we dive straight into key signatures, let's remind ourselves of the circle of fifths.

CIRCLE OF FIFTHS

- The circle of fifths is your essential diagram for all things theory.

- The circle of fifths is quite literally a circle that shows all 12 major and minor keys. The circle is broken up into 12 sections, one for each pitch in the chromatic scale. It also resembles a clock face, which makes it very easy to read.

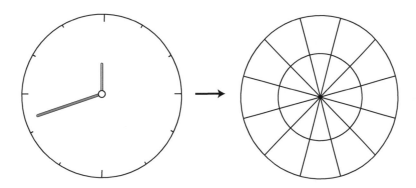

Clockwise round the circle

- The circle shows all 12 notes of the chromatic scale and moves clockwise in fifths. There are 12 pitches in Western music, hence why we have 12 sections on the circle.

- When we talk about a fifth, we literally mean five notes up from your starting note. Take a look at the scale below to see what that means.

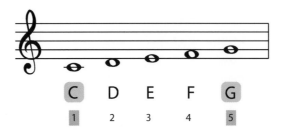

- As you can see, G is five notes above C. This means the next scale on the circle will be G major.

Anti-Clockwise round the circle

To work out the scales anti-clockwise on the circle, there are two different methods that we could use.

Method 1

- Count up in fourths.

- For example:

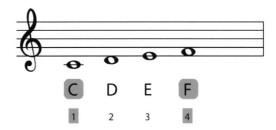

- F major will be the next scale anti-clockwise on the circle.

Method 2

- Count backwards five notes.

- This may be easier to visualise, but does require you to confidently know the different scales backwards.

- For example:

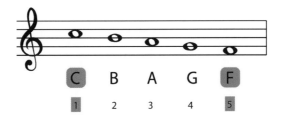

- Take a look at the circle of fifths below to see all the major scales inserted using this pattern of 5ths/4ths.

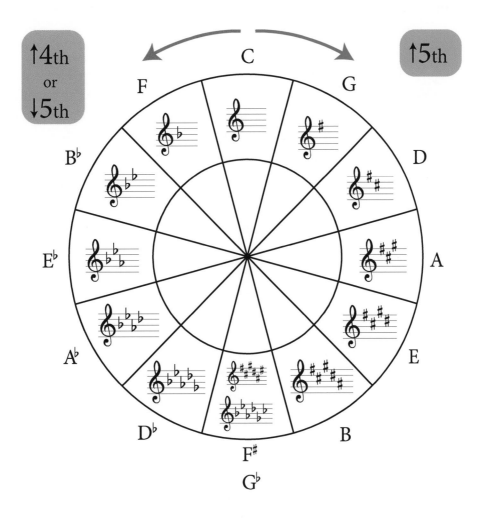

What goes in the middle of the circle?

- In the middle of the circle we always write in the **Relative Minor Scales**.

Key Fact

- Every major scale has a relative minor scale. Both of these scales share the same key signature.

- There are three different types of minor scale:

- **Natural Minor** – this minor scale shares its key signature with its relative major scale and is built starting on the sixth degree of that major scale. Both the major and relative natural minor will share the same key signature with no changes.

- **Harmonic Minor** – this minor scale also shares its key signature with the relative major scale and is built starting on the sixth degree of that major scale. However, to play the harmonic version of the minor scale you will have to raise the seventh degree by a semitone. We do this both ascending and descending.

- **Melodic Minor** – this minor scale shares its key signature with the relative major scale and is built starting on the sixth degree of that major scale. However, to play the melodic version of the minor scale, we need to raise the sixth and seventh degrees by a semitone when ascending and lower the sixth and seventh degrees by a semitone when descending. Note that on the way down we have the natural minor version of the scale.

- In order to find out the relative minor to each of these major scales, you must go to the 6th note of the major scale.

- Let's take a look at an example:

- The 6th note of C major is A natural. This means the relative minor of C major is A minor. Both scales will share the same key signature.

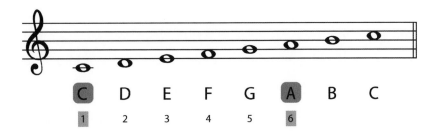

- Let's try another example.

- The 6th note of A major is F sharp. This means the relative minor of A major is F sharp minor. Both scales will share the same key signature.

Key Facts

- Remember that each Major scale has a relative Minor scale. Both of these scales share **the same** key signature.

- A key signature is always written in the **same** order.

- At the top of the circle of fifths is always the key/scale of C major. C major is always at the top because this scale has no sharps or flats.

- If we move one step clockwise on the circle of fifths, the next scale will have one sharp, the next step will then add a second sharp and so on and so forth. Gradually the sharps add up one at a time.

- We always keep the same sharp from the previous scale and just keep adding to the end.

- If we make one step anti clockwise on the circle of fifths, the next scale will have one flat, the next step will then add a second flat and so on and so forth. Gradually the flats add up one at a time.

- We always keep the same flat from the previous scale and just keep adding to the end.

- This is extremely useful when you are trying to work out what key your piece is written in. For example, if you see a key signature of three flats, you will know you are playing in the key of E flat major. As long as you have learnt the circle of fifths!

Major Key	Key Signature	Accidentals
C		
F		B♭
B♭		B♭ E♭
E♭		B♭ E♭ A♭
A♭		B♭ E♭ A♭ D♭
D♭		B♭ E♭ A♭ D♭ G♭
G♭		B♭ E♭ A♭ D♭ G♭ C♭

Major Key	Key Signature	Accidentals
C		
G		F♯
D		F♯ C♯
A		F♯ C♯ G♯
E		F♯ C♯ G♯ D♯
B		F♯ C♯ G♯ D♯ A♯
F♯		F♯ C♯ G♯ D♯ A♯ C♯

Here we have the complete Circle of Fifths with Major scales and Minor scales included.

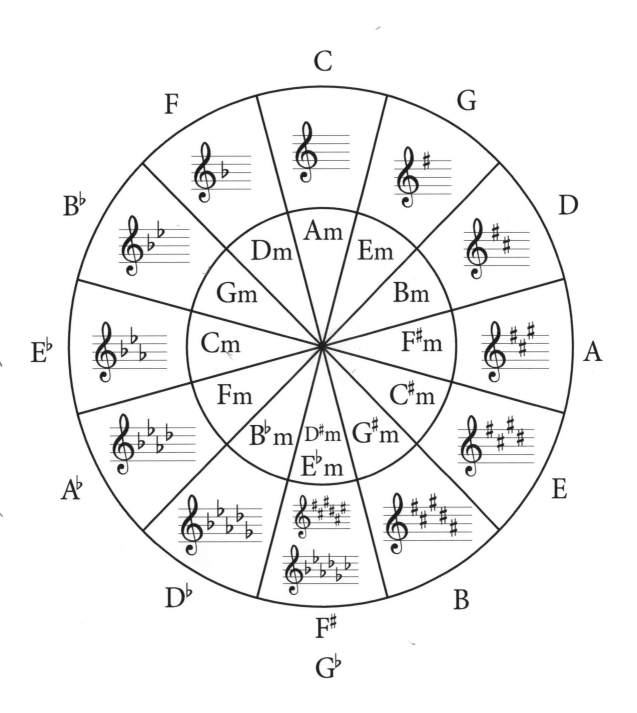

ENHARMONIC EQUIVALENTS

- There are two major and two minor scales in the bottom segment of the circle of fifths.

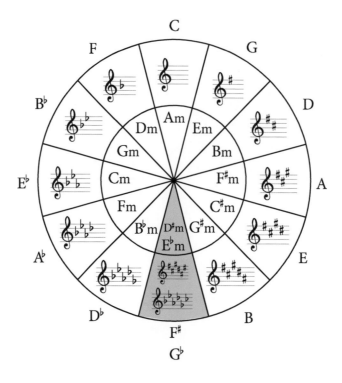

- F sharp major and D sharp minor have six sharps and G flat major and E flat minor have six flats.

- Look at the piano below. What do you notice about both the notes G flat/F sharp and E flat/D sharp?

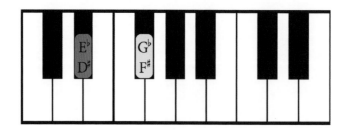

- They are both the same note on the piano! Due to the equal temperament tuning of the keyboard, this is what we call **Enharmonic Equivalents.**

Key Fact

- Enharmonic Equivalents are two pitches that sound the same but are notated differently (given a different letter). For example, F sharp and G flat, G sharp and A flat, C sharp and D flat etc.

MOVING BETWEEN ENHARMONIC EQUIVALENT SCALES

- For Grade 5 it is important to be confident moving between the Enharmonic Equivalent scales.

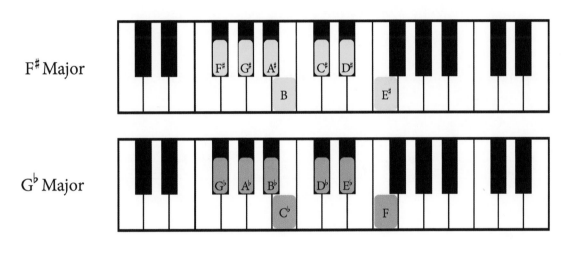

Notice how F# Major and Gb Major contain the same notes.

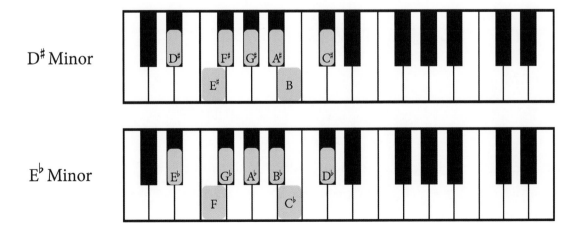

Notice how D# Minor and Eb Minor contain the same notes.

- Always start with the key signature. If you have a key signature of six sharps, this then needs to be changed to a key signature of six flats.

- This is because the key signature of six sharps is for F sharp major. F sharp's enharmonic equivalent note is G flat. G flat major has six flats, so this will be our new key signature.

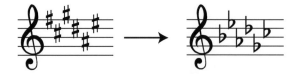

- Then you can change the rest of the notes, finding the enharmonic equivalent for each one.

- For example, if you are changing a piece from F sharp major to G flat major, all notes in the melody should be moved up by one note.

- If you are going from G flat major to F sharp major, all notes in the melody should be moved down by one note.

Moving from F# Major to Gb Major

Key Fact

- Remember that rather than looking at each note individually and working out its enharmonic equivalent, it is much easier to change the key signature and then move each note by the same interval.

CHROMATIC SCALES

- The final type of scale you need to know for the Grade 5 theory exam is the chromatic scale. The two types of scale you have learnt previously, major and minor, are what we call diatonic scales, meaning that they stay in a specific key. If you play a note that is outside of the specified key then these notes are called 'chromatic'. Chromatic simply means coloured, so it makes sense that these notes outside of your given key add colour to the music.

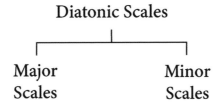

- A chromatic scale is one that is made up of these colourful notes, otherwise known as semitones. If you relate this to the piano, you would play all of the black and the white keys.

- The chromatic scale covers all 12 available pitches and when writing it out you will write out a total of 13 notes, as the first and last note will be the same.

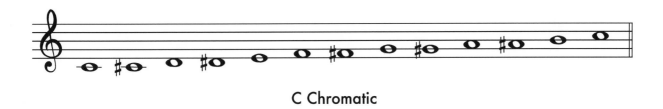

C Chromatic

- These scales move up in semitones and when written out, every line and every space will have a note on it. If you play the piano this is easy to visualise as it is all white and black keys.

- It is important that the first and last note use the same letter. You should remember that we cannot use enharmonic equivalents. For example, A sharp and B flat are enharmonic equivalents, but if your chromatic scale began on an A sharp then it should also finish on an A sharp.

A# B C C# D D# E F F# G G# A A#

- For the grade 5 exam you must ensure that you do not use the same letter more than twice. For example, A flat - A natural - A sharp. This is a chromatic sequence, but in order to achieve high marks in the exam you would need to replace one of these notes with the enharmonic equivalent. The note A flat could become G sharp, or alternatively A sharp could become B flat.

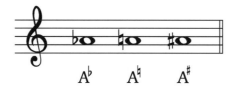

$A^\flat$ $A^\natural$ $A^\sharp$

- One important thing to check when writing out or double checking a chromatic scale is that you have not accidentally repeated a note by using its enharmonic equivalent.

B $C^\flat$ C   B C $D^\flat$

Incorrect   Correct

- You should also remember that if you have an accidental this will apply to the notes after it, so be sure to add or cancel accidentals as necessary.

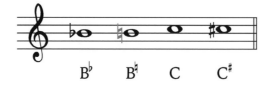

$B^\flat$ $B^\natural$ C $C^\sharp$

- We have to include the natural sign on the second B. If we did not do this, there would be two B flats and the sequence would not be chromatic.

TRANSPOSITION

For Grade 5 theory you need to be confident transposing by a:

- Major 2nd – up and down

- Perfect 5th – up and down

- Minor 3rd – up and down

Transposition is an essential skill, especially in the case of transposing instruments. There are some very common ones that you will know.

- Clarinet in Bb

- Alto Saxophone in Eb

- Trumpet in Bb

And many more…

What is a transposing instrument?

- A transposing instrument is where the note written for that instrument to play, is different to the note that we, as an audience, hear.

- For example, if you are playing the clarinet and you read the note C natural, the note that we will actually hear is a B flat. Similarly, when the Alto Saxophone plays a C natural, the note that we will actually hear is an E flat.

- In order to understand the music written down on the page and how it corresponds to what we hear, it is essential that we learn to transpose.

Key fact

- Any instrument whose music is notated at a different pitch to what it actually sounds, is what we call a transposing instrument.

Why do we need to learn about transposition?

- We need to learn how to transpose so we understand our instruments, understand the players around us and also know how to correctly notate and compose music for these instruments.

- Below is an example of what a Clarinet in Bb player will see on their music (written pitch) and what we as listeners will actually hear (sounding pitch).

Clarinet in Bb

Written Pitch

Sounding Pitch

Why do we have transposing instruments?

- The main reason for instruments being in different keys is to facilitate the ease of swapping between them. For example, in the saxophone family we have the Soprano, Alto, Tenor and Baritone Saxophone, to name but a few. Due to each instrument being made in a different key, it means that the player can use the same fingering for every instrument, even though the sounding pitches will be different.

- For example:

Soprano Saxophone: This saxophone is in the key of B flat. Therefore, if you were to play a C, the sounding pitch would be a B flat.

Alto Saxophone: This saxophone is in the key of E flat. Again, if you were to play a C, the sounding pitch would be an E flat.

Before we can work up to transposing between different keys, we need to fully understand how notes can be written using different clefs. Visit the Clefs chapter to make sure you have a strong understanding.

TRANSPOSING DOWN A MAJOR 2ND

- Major second transposition is used for instruments in the key of B flat, such as the Clarinet in Bb.

- When we move from written pitch to sounding pitch, we must transpose **down** a major 2nd and when we go from sounding pitch to written pitch we must transpose **up** a major 2nd.

- Below is a simple melody in C major. We know that this melody is in C major, as the key signature contains no sharps or flats.

- We need to transpose this down a major second in order for us to see what the sounding pitch of the melody is.

- We could look at each note individually but this would take a long time. The easiest thing to do is change the key signature first. But how do we work out what a major second lower than C major is?

Key fact

- A major second is the same as a **Tone** (2 semitones).

- What is a tone (two semitones) lower than C natural? Take a look at the piano below...

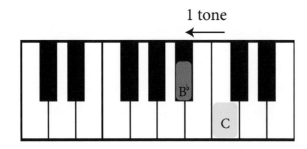

- B flat is a tone lower than C natural.

- Check that your answer is a major second lower by asking, **is C natural in B flat major?**

- C natural **is** in B flat major!

- Now let's go back to our short melody.

- We need to change the key signature to a B flat major key signature. As we saw earlier, this will have two flats. If you are unsure why this is, please re-read the circle of fifths section in the scale and key signatures chapter.

Bb Major

- Once the key signature is changed we then need to move all of our notes down by a second.

- Below you can see the full transposition.

Transposition down a Major 2nd

Key Facts

- When transposing the key signature, ask yourself, is my top note in the major scale of my bottom note?

- Remember we always work out an interval by asking if the top note is in the scale of the bottom note and never the other way around.

TRANSPOSING UP A MAJOR 2ND

- The melody below is in A major, we know this because we have three sharps. This is the sounding pitch. We need to transpose this up a major second so that we can see the written pitch for the Clarinet in Bb.

- What note is a major 2nd (tone) higher than A natural?

1 tone

- It's a B natural.

- We can check that this is right by asking ourselves if B natural is in A major.

- B natural **is** in A major, so we now know that we will need a key signature of **five** sharps. This is because B major has five sharps. Below is our new key signature.

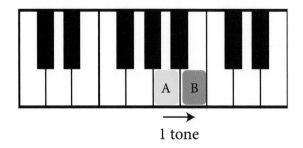

B Major

- We now need to move each note up by the interval of a second.

• Below you can see the full transposition:

Transposition up a Major 2nd

TRANSPOSING DOWN A PERFECT 5TH

- Perfect 5th transposition is used for transposing instruments that are in the key of F. The most common instrument in the key of F is the French horn.

- When we move from written pitch to sounding pitch, we must transpose **down** a perfect 5th and when we go from sounding pitch to written pitch we must transpose **up** a perfect 5th.

- Below we have a melody in the key of C major.

- What note is five notes below C natural?

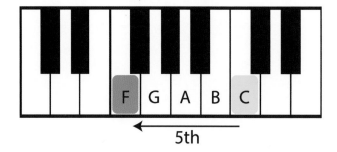

- It is F natural!

- We could also use the circle of fifths.

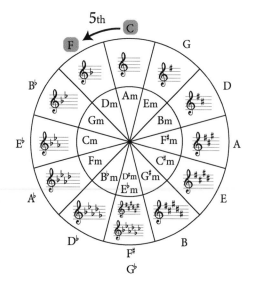

- We now know that F major will be our new transposed key. What is the key signature of F major?

- The key signature of F major has one flat. This flat must be B flat.

F Major

- Let's now apply this to our melody. Remember to change the key signature and then move each note down a 5th.

- Below you can see the full transposition.

Transposition down a Perfect 5th

TRANSPOSING UP A PERFECT 5TH

- What scale is the melody below written in?

- Four flats indicates that we are in the key of A flat major.

- What is a perfect fifth above A flat?

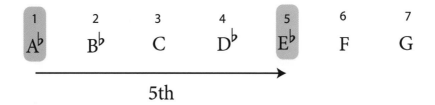

- A perfect 5th above A flat is E flat.

- Remember we could also use the circle of fifths.

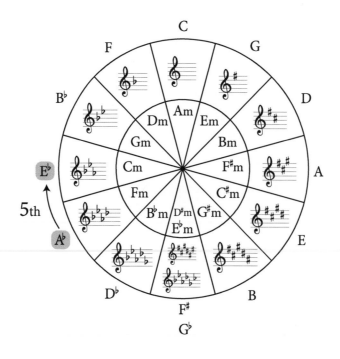

- We now know that E flat major will be our new transposed key. What is the key signature of E flat major?

- The key signature of E flat major is three flats. B flat, E flat and A flat.

Eb Major

- Now let's apply this to the melody. Remember to change the key signature and then move each note up a 5th.

- Below you can see the full transposition.

Transposition up a Perfect 5th

TRANSPOSING BY A MINOR 3RD

- When transposing by a Minor 3rd, we are thinking about instruments in the key of A. The most common being the Clarinet in A.

- When transposing up a Minor 3rd, we are going from sounding pitch to written pitch. When transposing down a Minor 3rd, we are going from written pitch to sounding pitch.

What is a Minor 3rd?

- Before moving on to the full transposition, how do we work out the Minor 3rd interval?

- Think about the two notes below.

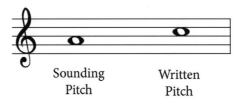

Sounding
Pitch

Written
Pitch

- We hear an A natural.

- We read a C natural.

- What is the interval between these two notes?

Key Fact

- Remember an interval simply means the distance between two notes.

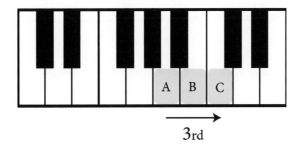

3rd

- We have three notes. This means we are looking at an interval of a 3rd, because the distance between the A and C is **three** notes.

Key Fact

- We do not need to count the sharps and flats between the notes to work out the interval's number. Simply focus on the letters... A, B, C. Three letters, three notes.

How do we know it is a Minor 3rd and not a Major 3rd?

- Remember when we are working out an interval, we always start with the lowest note of the two. Which one here is lower?

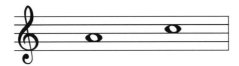

- A is the lower of the two notes. Below is the A major scale.

- Is C natural in A major? No it is not.

Key Fact

- A Minor third interval is one semitone smaller than a major third interval.

- What is one semitone smaller than C sharp?

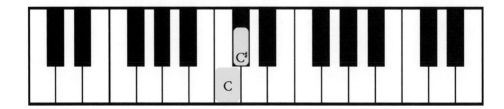

- C natural is one semitone smaller than C sharp. This is how we know that A natural to C natural is a minor 3rd.

- Another method is to simply write out the minor scale and see what the third is.

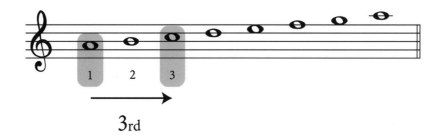

3rd

Key Facts

- In a minor scale, the interval of a 3rd is **always** a minor 3rd.

- In a major scale, the interval of a 3rd is **always** a major 3rd.

- Minor 3rd intervals are made up of 3 semitones.

TRANSPOSING DOWN A MINOR 3RD

- If we are transposing down a minor 3rd, we are going from written pitch to sounding pitch.

- Can we transpose the melody below down a minor 3rd? The melody below has the key signature of G major, but it would be better to think about this piece in its relative minor, E minor.

- We could look at each note individually and move them down by a minor 3rd, but this would take a long time. It would also involve working out lots of intervals, rather than transposing the whole piece in a quick and efficient way.

- To transpose the melody, we need to first change the key signature and then move the notes down a 3rd.

- We have the key signature of E minor in our original melody. What is a minor 3rd lower than E natural?

- Remember a minor 3rd is made up of 3 semitones. Look at the piano below.

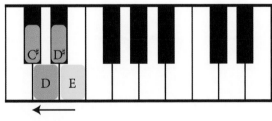

Down 3 Semitones

- As you can see, C sharp is 3 semitones lower than E natural. We can check this further by writing out the C sharp minor scale.

- The reason we write out the C sharp minor scale is because this is the lower note of the interval. To check that the interval is correct, you must always see if the higher note is in the scale of the lower note.

- The 3rd in a minor scale is always a Minor 3rd, so by writing out the C sharp minor scale, we can easily check if E natural is in the scale.

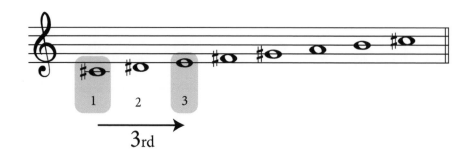

- Is E natural the third note? Yes it is! Therefore, you have gone down a minor third. Let's write out our new melody in C sharp minor.

- Below you can see the full transposition.

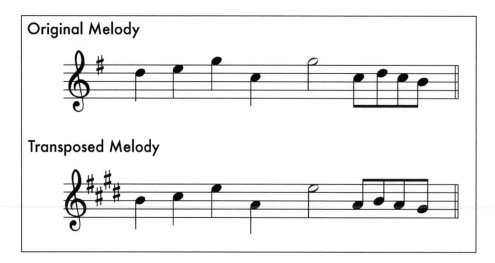

Transposition down a Minor 3rd

TRANSPOSING UP A MINOR 3RD

- When transposing up a minor 3rd we are going from sounding pitch to written pitch.

- Can we transpose this melody **up** a minor 3rd? What minor key is it written in?

- It is written in D minor. What is a minor 3rd (three semitones) higher than D?

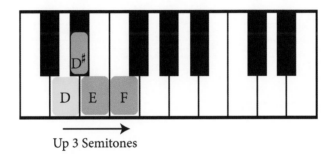

Up 3 Semitones

- F natural.

- What is the key signature of F minor?

- Remember F minor's relative major is A flat major, so we have four flats.

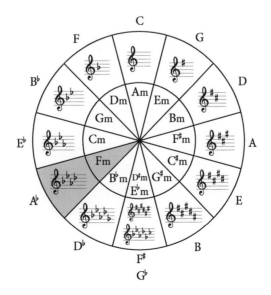

- The next step is to move all the notes in the melody up a 3rd. As you have already changed the key signature, you do not need to think about each note individually.

- Below you can see the full transposition.

Transposition up a Minor 3rd

Key Facts

- If you think about your key as a minor key, the scale you transpose to should also be a minor key.

- If you think in a major key, the scale you transpose to should also be a major key.

- To go down a minor 3rd, it is important to think in semitones to ensure accuracy. You can then check that the scale you have arrived at is the correct one by writing out the minor scale of the lower pitch and checking the third note.

TRANSPOSING ACCIDENTALS

- It is important to always think about your accidentals separately as often, simply changing the key signature will not ensure that you have the correct note.

- As with working out our key signatures, to find out if we have moved the correct interval, we must ask ourselves if the top note is in the scale of the bottom note.

- Let's start by transposing the below note down by a major 2nd. The sharp sign is an accidental.

- Let's put this note on the piano. Can you work out which note is a major 2nd lower than F sharp?

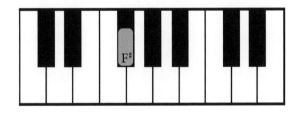

- Remember a tone (two semitones) is the same as a major 2nd.

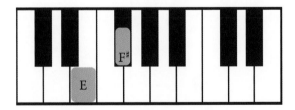

- E natural is a major 2nd lower.

- We can check. **Is F sharp in E major?** – YES!

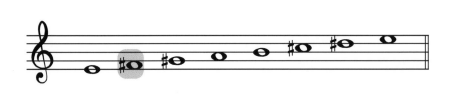

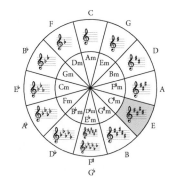

- When you put this note into your transposed melody you will need to put a natural sign next to the new note 'E'. Or, if there is no E flat or E sharp in the new key signature, you can simply leave the E without an accidental written at all.

Key Facts

- An accidental is a note that it not a member of the scale/key that your melody is written in.

- When you have an accidental in the melody, you need to treat it separately to the other notes. Work it out as a separate interval.

Sometimes an accidental can create a problem. What if you don't know the scale of the bottom note?

- Let's see if we can transpose this note up by a perfect 5th. The flat sign is an accidental.

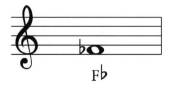

- What note is a 5th above F? Remember, when working out the interval's distance, you do not need to include the accidentals.

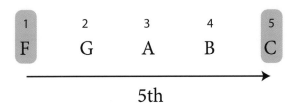

5th

- C is a **5th** above F. However, is **F flat** to C natural a perfect 5th?

- Do you know the scale of F flat major? This scale is not included on our Circle of Fifths! To make this easier bring the note F flat up a semitone to F natural. F natural is a much easier scale to understand. Now let's work out what a perfect 5th above F natural is.

- A 5th above F natural is C natural. We now need to bring this back down a semitone (remember we raised the F flat by a semitone at the beginning). This leaves us with C flat.

- C flat is a perfect 5th above F flat.

- The accidental you will now place on the C will be a flat sign.

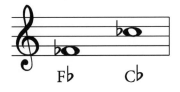

Perfect 5th

Key Fact

- If are transposing music that contains an accidental, make sure you treat this as a separate interval. More to come on intervals in the next chapter.

INTERVALS

REVISION FROM GRADES 1-4

- In Grades 1-4 you learnt how to work out the distance of an interval and how to label this with a descriptive word such as Major, Minor, Perfect, Diminished or Augmented.

- If that sentence sounds scary don't worry! Let's revise this before going onto the Grade 5 requirements.

Key Facts

- An interval is simply the difference between two pitches (or notes).

- Remember that the distance between every note that is next to each other or on top of each other is an interval.

- Think about your scales. The distance between every note is an interval.

An interval can be considered either Melodic or Harmonic.

Melodic Interval

- A melodic interval is where the notes are played successively.

Harmonic Interval

- A harmonic interval is where the notes are played simultaneously.

How do we work out the intervals number?

- An interval is always labelled with a number and in order to work out the intervals number we have to see what the distance between the two notes is.

- Make sure you are very clear about the degrees of the scale.

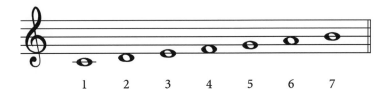

- Once clear about the degrees of the scale, it will be much easier to work out the distance of your interval. The degrees of the scale start on the first note; this means that we must include the starting note when working out our intervals.

- What is the distance between the two notes in the melodic interval below?

59

- How do we count this correctly?

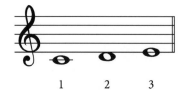

- E is the 3rd degree of the C scale. The difference between middle C and E is 3. This makes this an interval of a 3rd!

- Let's try a harmonic interval.

- Here we have a G and a C. Which degree of the G scale is the note C ?

- C is the 4th degree, meaning the distance from G to C is 4. This is the interval of a 4th.

How do we know the interval's descriptive word?

- Each interval is also labelled with a description. This could be Major, Minor, or Perfect. There are two more, but we will revise these main three first.

- What is the interval (distance) between the two notes below?

- Remember, we always work the interval out by going from bottom to top. The bottom note is G. Below is the scale of G major.

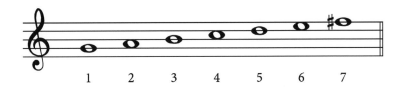

- B is the 3rd note of G major and this makes the interval a 3rd. In order to work out whether this is a Major or Minor interval we need to see if the top note is in the scale of the bottom note. Is B natural in G major?

- B natural **is** in G major, making this interval a Major 3rd.

- The Minor 3rd is one semitone smaller than a Major 3rd. Let's look at the piano below.

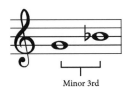

back 1 semitone

- One semitone smaller than a B natural is a B flat meaning that the interval written below (G natural - B flat) is a minor 3rd!

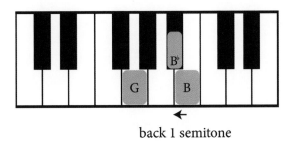

Minor 3rd

Key Fact

- We always work out the interval from the bottom note up, regardless of which way round the notes are written.

61

Let's try one more example

- The lowest note in this interval is the second note, which is D natural.

- What is the interval between D natural and B flat?

- The interval is a 6th. Is B flat in D major?

- D major has a B natural. B flat is a semitone smaller than B natural, making this a Minor 6th!

Minor 6th

There are three intervals that cannot be considered major or minor

- These are the intervals of a **4th, 5th** and **8ve.** For these three intervals, we use the word Perfect.

Key Facts

- The word **Perfect** is used because the 4th, 5th and 8ve are the same in both the major and minor scale so therefore cannot be labelled as major or minor.

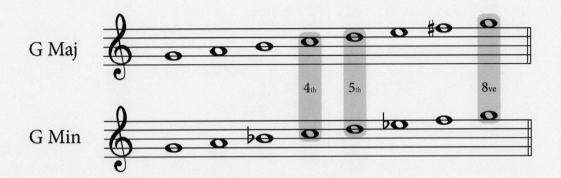

- As you can clearly see, the 4th, 5th and 8ve are all the same!

- Let's have a look at the interval below.

- This interval would simply be called a Perfect 5th!

Augmented and Diminished Intervals

- On top of the descriptions Major, Minor and Perfect, we also have the descriptive words Diminished and Augmented.

- Have a look at the diagram below:

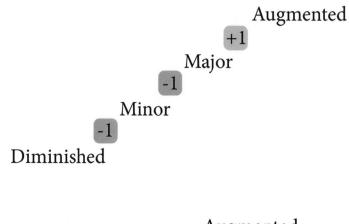

- We have two separate diagrams, one for the Major/Minor intervals (2nd, 3rd, 6th and 7th) and one for the Perfect intervals (4th, 5th and 8ve).

- Both categories can have Augmented or Diminished intervals.

AUGMENTED INTERVALS

- An Augmented interval is **one** semitone larger than a Major or Perfect interval.

- Above, we have the interval of F natural to A sharp.

- Is A sharp in F major? A sharp is not in F major. F major contains an A natural.

- If we use the piano, we can work out how many semitones we have gone up to reach A sharp.

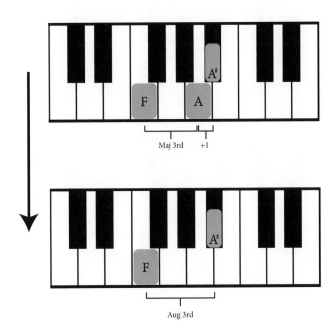

- We have gone up by one semitone from the Major interval. This makes this interval an Augmented 3rd.

Let's try another example

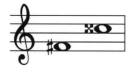

- Here we have an F sharp followed by a C double sharp.

- Is C double sharp in F sharp major? No, it is not. In F sharp major we have a C sharp.

- We can use the piano again to help us work out how many semitones we have gone up to get to C double sharp.

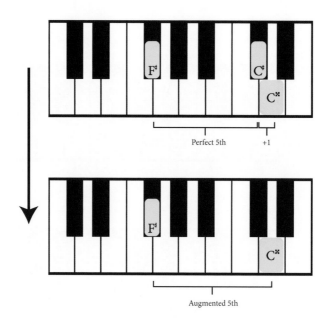

- We have gone up one semitone from C sharp to C double sharp. This makes this interval an Augmented 5th.

DIMINISHED INTERVALS

- A Diminished interval is **one** semitone smaller than a Minor or Perfect interval.

- Let's have a look at the interval below:

- We have a G natural to E double flat.

- Is E double flat in G major?

- No, it is not. In G major we have an E natural.

- How many semitones lower is E double flat than E natural?

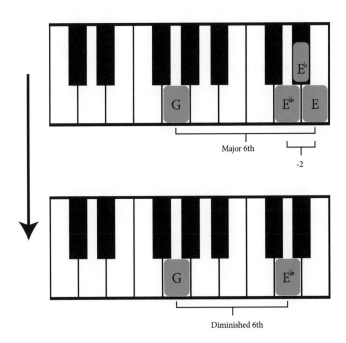

- E double flat is two semitones lower than E natural. This makes this interval a Diminished 6th.

But what do I do if I don't know the scale of the bottom note?

- Sometimes you will be given a question where you simply do not know the scale of the bottom note.

- Look at this interval below:

- G sharp major is an extremely difficult scale and not included on our circle of fifths... I bet you can't tell me how many sharps are in it?!

- Rather than struggling through and trying to figure out how many sharps are in G sharp major, let's bring this note down a semitone to G natural.

Key Fact

- Remember, if you bring the bottom note down a semitone then you must also bring the top note down by a semitone as well to keep the interval the same. Always do the same to the top as you do to the bottom.

- If we bring the lower note (G sharp) down a semitone, we must also bring the upper note (D natural) down a semitone as well. Bringing D natural down a semitone takes us to D flat.

- Here is the new interval:

- This is an easier interval to work out. So, what is the distance between these two notes?

- The interval is a 5th. Is D flat in G major?

- D flat is not in G major; there is a D natural in G major. Therefore, we have come down by a semitone. G natural to D natural would have been a Perfect 5th, so G natural to D flat is a Diminished 5th!

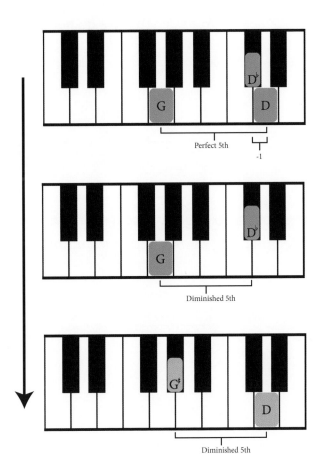

Let's try another example

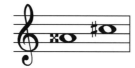

- A double sharp major; this is definitely a scale that we do not know.

- Let's bring both notes down a semitone.

- We now have got to A sharp. A sharp major is also a scale that most of us would feel uncomfortable using. Let's bring it down by another semitone.

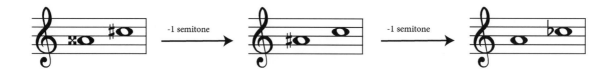

- We have now landed at the note A. A major is a much more well known scale and one we are all comfortable with.

- We have come down two semitones so we need to make sure we do the same to the top note. What is two semitones lower than C sharp?

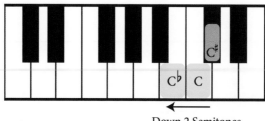

Down 2 Semitones

- Two semitones lower than C sharp is C flat.

- Here is our new interval.

- What is the distance between these two notes?

- The distance between A natural and C natural is a 3rd. Remember to work out the distance between two notes you do not need to worry about the accidentals.

- Is C flat in A major? Take a look at A major scale below.

- C flat is not in A major. In A major we have a C sharp – how many semitones have we come down?

- We have come down by two semitones. Two semitones down from a Major interval brings us to a Diminished interval.

- The answer to this question is a **Diminished 3rd.**

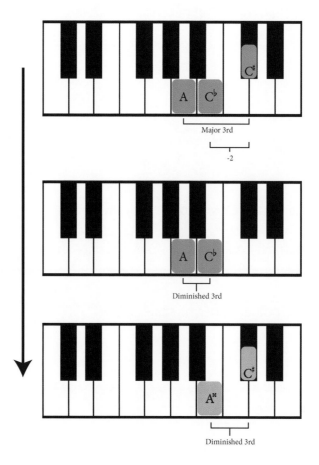

- As A natural to C sharp is a Diminished 3rd, so too is our original interval of A double sharp to C sharp.

COMPOUND INTERVALS

- Make sure you are really confident with all of the above before visiting this section. In Grade 5 you need to be confident recognising all intervals, including Compound intervals.

- A Compound interval is one that is larger than an octave.

- What do we do if we need to find an interval that is larger than an octave? There are two ways to approach this.

Method 1

- We can simply continue to count on.

- What is the distance between these two notes?

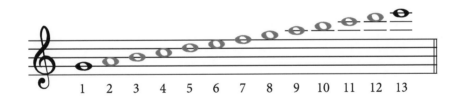

- The distance between these two notes is a 13th.

- We can now ask ourselves the usual question: is the top note in the scale of the bottom note?

- Is E natural in G major?

- E natural **is** in G major.

- This makes this interval a Major 13th.

- However, this is not the only way to describe this interval. Another way of looking at this involves using the word **Compound.**

Method 2

- Compound simply means 'larger than an octave'.

- Let's look at the interval from Method 1.

- This interval would be far easier to work out if the E natural were an octave lower. Let's put this interval back to its simple state i.e. E natural, one octave lower to make the total distance in the interval less than an octave.

- This would now be an interval of a 6th. Is E natural in G major? Yes it is! This is therefore a Major 6th.

- Back to the original interval…

- The original interval is larger than one octave. We worked out that the simple version of the interval was a Major 6th. In order to show that the actual interval is larger than an octave we can simply put the word compound at the start. Therefore the interval is a **Compound Major 6th.**

Key Facts

- There are two different ways to label an interval larger than an octave.

- This can be naming the literal distance between the two notes (9th, 10th, 11th etc) or working out what the interval would be if it was in its simple state and then writing the word Compound in front of it.

- Both ways achieve the exact same answer.

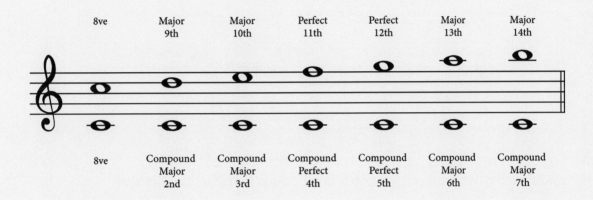

- It is also important to consider which intervals will be Perfect and which will be Major/Minor.

- In our simple intervals, the 4th, 5th and 8ve are Perfect. If you are using the Compound method then this rule still applies – easy!

- If you are using method 1, where you are simply counting the literal distance, then you must remember that the intervals of an 11th and 12th will be Perfect.

Let's try an example using method 1:

- What interval do we have here?

- For this example we will use Method 1 (finding the literal distance between the notes).

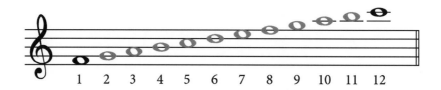

- The distance between these two notes is a 12th. Is C natural in F major?

- C natural **is** in F major.

- Remember that if we have an interval of a 12th, this will be **Perfect**.

- The answer to this question (using method 1) will therefore be a **Perfect 12th.**

Let's try an example using method 2:

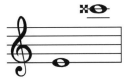

- For this example, we will use method 2.

- Firstly, we need to bring the interval to its simple state.

- What is the distance between these two notes?

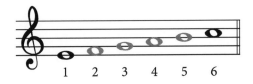

- The distance is a 6th. Is C double sharp in E major?

- C double sharp is not in E major, but there is a C sharp. C double sharp is just one semitone larger than C sharp, making this interval an **Augmented 6th.**

- Don't forget the word compound.

- The final answer is a **Compound Augmented 6th.**

CHORDS

WHAT IS A CHORD?

- A chord is a set of notes/pitches that are played simultaneously (at the same time).

- Chords are usually made up of three different pitches.

Triads

- A chord with three different pitches is called a triad.

- Triads consist of the root, the third above that and then the fifth above that.

- These intervals help to determine whether your chord is Major, Minor, Diminished or Augmented.

- The most common triads are:

    - Major Triad – major third and a perfect fifth above the root.

    - Minor Triad – minor third and a perfect fifth above the root.

    - Diminished Triad – minor third and a diminished fifth above the root.

    - Augmented Triad – major third and an augmented fifth above the root.

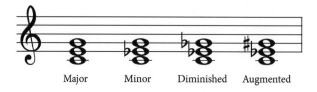

Triads in C Major

- Remember - any of these pitches can be doubled, without changing the name of the chord, as long as the root stays the same.

WRITING CHORDS

- Before you can create a chord, it is important to know the scale you are in first. Let's look at the below G major scale, we know this is a G major scale due to its key signature of one sharp.

- It is possible to easily create a chord on each note of the scale. We will end up with seven different triads. These triads are only made up of notes in the scale of G major.

- As you can see, a chord is created using the bottom note or 'root' and then placing two more notes on top, a third above the root and a fifth above the root.

- Notice that these chords are either written all on lines or all in spaces.

Key Facts

- Remember it is important to use Roman Numerals to identify your chords. A chord is built on the degree of the scale which gives us the number of the chord.

I	II	III	IV	V	VI	VII
1	2	3	4	5	6	7

- A chord is always defined firstly by the key you are in and then by its root.

HOW DO WE LABEL CHORDS?

- In order to effectively label chords, it is important that you are confident with key signatures as you cannot label a chord without knowing what key/scale you are in.

- If you are not confident with your key signatures, make sure to re-read the scales and key signatures chapter and practice drawing out the circle of fifths.

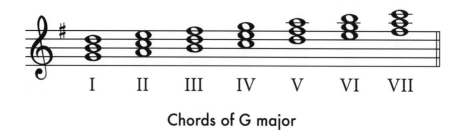

Chords of G major

- Take a look at the chords above. Notice that the chord that starts on G, the first chord in the scale, is called Chord I. The next chord after this is Chord II and so on and so forth.

- If we were to have a key signature of two sharps instead, this would then indicate that we are in the key of D major. This would mean that all of the chords would change. Chord I would now start on a D, Chord II on an E etc.

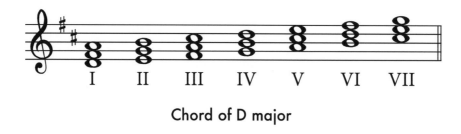

Chord of D major

- We can also be faced with a minor scale. In order to recognise this you must watch out for accidentals. Remember a minor scale shares its key signature with the relative major, but you will also have a raised seventh note to indicate that you are in the harmonic minor scale. For example what scale do we have below?

- We have a key signature of one flat, indicating that we are in F major. However, as you can see there is a C sharp meaning that this is the relative minor of F major, D minor.

- This will then change the chords as you can see below.

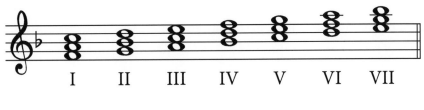

Chords of F major

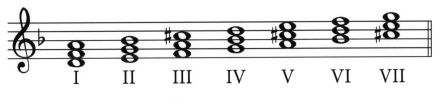

Chords of D minor

Chords for Grade 5

- For Grade 5 you must be confident with the following chords in all keys:

  Chord I = Tonic

  Chord ii = Supertonic

  Chord IV = Subdominant

  Chord V = Dominant

- Chords I, IV and V are **Major** triads. This is true for all scales.

- Chord ii will always be a **Minor** triad. This is true for all scales.

Key Facts

- **You may see other chord labels on your music. These are explained below, but are not strictly required for Grade 5. We have included them for completeness.**

- If the interval of a third in your chord is major, you need to write the roman numerals in capital letters, indicating to the performer that the chord is major.

- If the interval of a third in your chord is minor, you will need to write the roman numerals in lowercase letters, indicating to the performer that the chord is minor.

- If the interval of a fifth in your chord is perfect, then you do not need to add any extra labelling.

- If the interval of a fifth in your chord is diminished, then you need to draw a small circle at the top right of the roman numeral. You will have seen this a lot in the case of chord vii in your scales, as this chord is always diminished.

- If the interval of a fifth in your chord is augmented then you need to draw a small plus sign at the top right of the roman numeral.

CHORD INVERSIONS

- In Grade 5 you must also be comfortable with chord inversions. The three main inversions are:

    - Root position

    - First inversion

    - Second inversion

Root position

- Root position is the usual position of the chord. It is where the chord has its root at the bottom. The root is the home note of the chord.

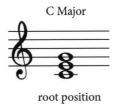

First Inversion

- First inversion is when the 3rd of the chord is put at the bottom (the second note of the chord). This is called the 1st inversion.

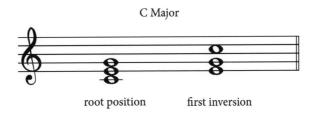

Second Inversion

- Second inversion is when the 5th of the chord is put at the bottom (the third note of the chord). This is called the 2nd inversion.

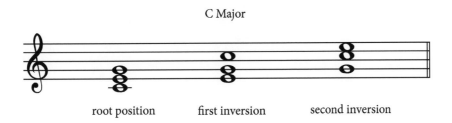

Use the following method to label inversions

- For a root position chord we place the letter 'a' next to the chord's number.

- For a first inversion chord we place the letter 'b' next to the chord's number.

- For a second inversion chord we place the letter 'c' next to the chord's number.

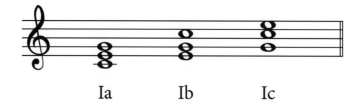

Ia   Ib   Ic

Key Fact

- When writing out the root position chord, the 'a' is very often omitted.

Alternative method

- Chords can also be labelled by using what we call **figured bass**.

- Figured bass is an alternative method for labelling your chords. The numbers literally indicate the interval above the root.

- A root position chord would be labelled as   5
                                              3

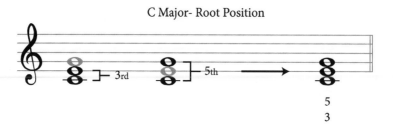

C Major- Root Position

- A first inversion chord would be labelled as $\begin{matrix}6\\3\end{matrix}$

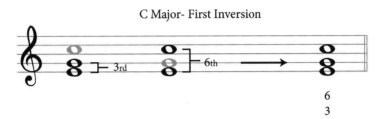

- A second inversion chord would be labelled as $\begin{matrix}6\\4\end{matrix}$

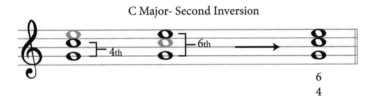

CADENCES

- A cadence is a sequence of chords put at the end of a phrase.

- A cadence is able to make a phrase sound finished, unfinished or end with a surprise!

Key Fact

- A phrase is a single unit of music that makes complete sense on its own. They are usually 2, 4 or 8 bars in length. A phrase will always end in a cadence.

- The three most important cadences to understand for Grade 5 are:

Cadence	Chords
Perfect	V-I
Plagal	IV-I
Imperfect	I-V or II-V or IV-V

- In general, perfect and plagal cadences sound finished and an imperfect cadence sounds unfinished.

- Working out a cadence is very much like working out chords; we use the same principles. Remember a cadence is just a sequence of chords next to each other.

HOW TO CHOOSE CHORDS FOR YOUR CADENCE

- Make sure that you recognise the key by looking at the key signature and accidentals very carefully.

- Choose a chord that contains the notes in that phrase.

- If you have accidentals then it is likely the key you are looking for is a minor scale. For example, if you have a F sharp in the key signature but you have D sharps in the melody, then you are not in G major, but rather in E minor (D sharp is E minor's raised seventh).

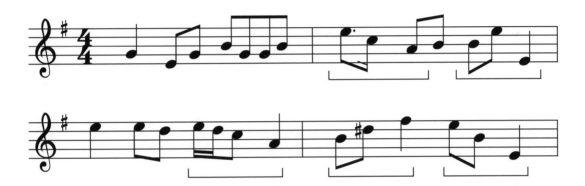

- Write out the chords I, II, IV and V in the key of E Minor.

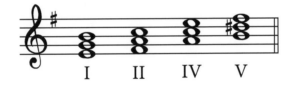

- Look carefully at the notes in the melody. Which chords do the majority of the bracketed notes fit into?

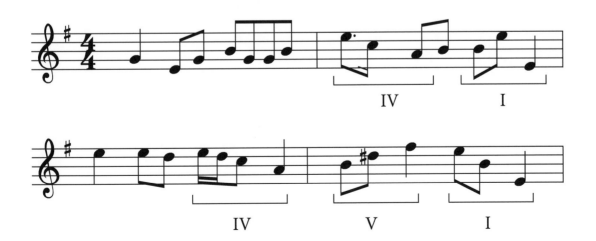

87

Key Facts

- The last two chords of the sequence can only be one of the above cadences, so if your first chord is V, you can safely say the next chord will be chord I. And if your first chord is I or II, you can safely say the last chord will be V. If you first chord is IV, then this will either be followed by chord I or V.

- The two chords you choose for the cadence must form a plagal, perfect or imperfect cadence.

- If the last chord in your melody only includes one note, you have to make sure the chord you choose fits within the cadence. It will either be chord I or V.

- A cadence only includes two chords, but in the Grade 5 exam you may be asked to insert a chord before a cadence (making a sequence of three chords). For this extra chord choose either chord I, II, IV or V depending on which one best matches the highlighted notes.

INSTRUMENTS OF THE ORCHESTRA

The orchestra is divided into different families:

String Family – these instruments are played with a bow or plucked.

Woodwind Family – these instruments are blown. They will use a reed or a simple open hole you blow over.

Brass Family – these instruments are blown. However, for these instruments you vibrate your lips into a mouthpiece.

Percussion Family – These instruments are played with beaters, sticks or simply hit with the hand.

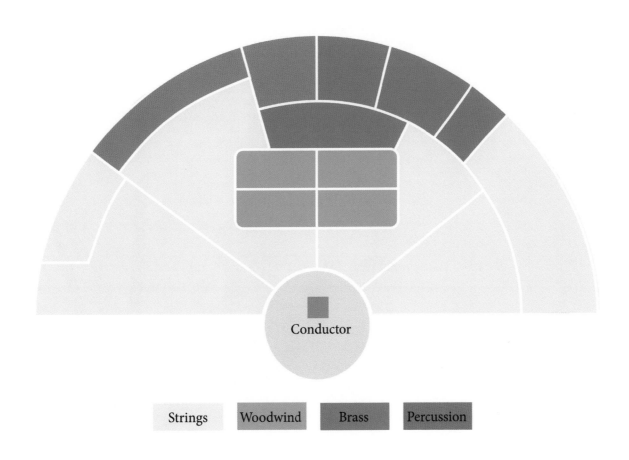

STRING FAMILY

Instrument	Clef	Transposing	How is it played?	Other Information
Violin	𝄞	No	Bow or plucked	Four strings.
Viola	𝄡	No	Bow or plucked	Four strings.
Cello	𝄢	No	Bow or plucked	Four strings.
Double Bass	𝄢	No	Bow or plucked	Four strings.
Harp	𝄞 𝄢	No	Plucked	Has 47 strings and plays two lines of music like the piano. Pedals are also pressed by the feet to change the pitch of the strings.

Violin   Viola   Cello   Double Bass   Harp

WOODWIND FAMILY

Instrument	Clef	Transposing	How is it played?	Other Information
Piccolo	𝄞	No	Air blown over lip plate.	A smaller version of the flute, but an octave higher.
Flute	𝄞	No	Air blown over lip plate.	
Oboe	𝄞	No	Air blown into a double reed.	
Cor Anglais	𝄞	Yes	Air blown into a double reed.	A larger version of the oboe, also known as the English Horn.
Clarinet	𝄞	Yes	Air blown into a single reed.	
Bassoon	𝄢	No	Air blown into a double reed.	

Key Facts

Single reed – thin piece of wood, placed on a mouthpiece where it vibrates against it. The most common orchestral instrument to use a single reed is the Clarinet.

Double reed – two thin pieces of wood which are bound together. The two thin pieces of wood vibrate against each other to produce a sound. The most common orchestral instruments to use double reeds are the Oboe, Cor Anglais and Bassoon.

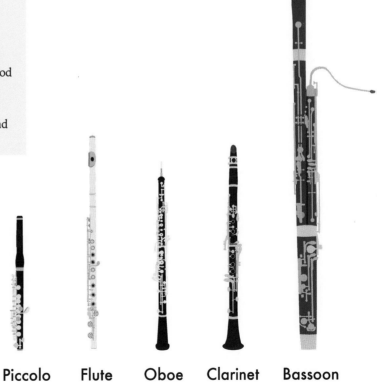

Piccolo　Flute　Oboe　Clarinet　Bassoon

BRASS FAMILY

Instrument	Clef	Transposing	How is it played?	Other Information
Trumpet	𝄞	Yes	Vibrating lips into mouthpiece.	In the key of Bb.
French Horn	𝄞	Yes	Vibrating lips into mouthpiece.	The mouthpiece on a french horn is the smallest out of all of the brass instruments. In the key of F.
Trombone	𝄢	No	Vibrating lips into mouthpiece.	Much larger mouthpiece than the trumpet or french horn.
Tuba	𝄢	No	Vibrating lips into mouthpiece.	Largest mouthpiece of all the brass instruments.

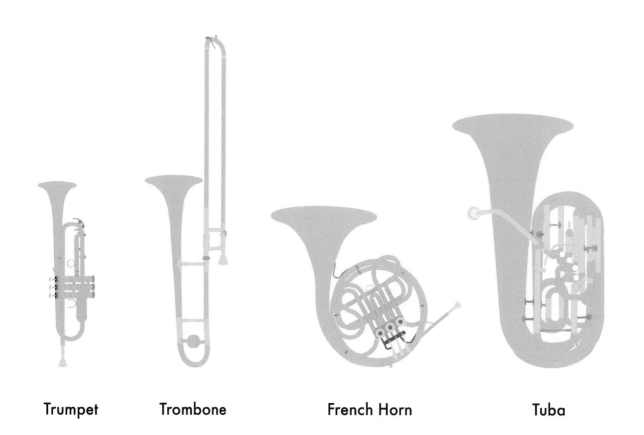

Trumpet   Trombone   French Horn   Tuba

PERCUSSION FAMILY

Instrument	Other Information
Timpani	This instrument is also referred to as the kettledrum. It is a large drum that has a membrane stretched over a metal bowl. The drum can be tuned using the pedals and is struck with a beater. The player will usually have a few drums as each drum can only play one pitch.
Tubular Bells	The tubular bells are made up of large, vertical metal bars. The bells are tuned by altering the length and the sound is made to duplicate the sound of church bells. It is struck with hard beaters.
Xylophone	The xylophone consists of horizontal wooden bars that are struck with wooden beaters. The pitch of the notes varies depending on the size of the wooden bar.
Marimba	The marimba is very similar to the xylophone in that it consists of wooden bars, but underneath you will find pipes to amplify the sound. The wooden bars are struck with rubber mallets and the pitch of the notes varies depending on the size of each wooden bar. The instrument is played using soft beaters.
Glockenspiel	Like the xylophone, the glockenspiel consists of horizontal bars, but these bars are made of metal. The bars are struck with beaters and the pitch varies depending on the size of the bar.
Vibraphone	This instrument is similar to the glockenspiel in that the bars are made of metal but rather than just relying on being struck, it also contains a motor to add vibration to the sound.
Celesta	The celesta looks very much like a piano but it is smaller in size. Inside there are metal bars which gives it its charactersitic bell sound.
Snare Drum	This drum is also known as the side drum. It is struck with a beater and produces a strong, sharp sound. This is due to the stiff wires stretched underneath the drum. These wires vibrate when the drum is struck to produce its unique sound.
Bass Drum	A large drum that produces a low pitch when struck with a mallet or beater.
Cymbals	Cymbals often come in pairs and consist of thin, gold discs. Cymbals can be struck with a beater or crashed together! They have many unique uses in an orchestra.
Tambourine	The tambourine is small and drum-like in shape. Around the edge of the instrument are small gold discs called 'zills'. The tambourine can be struck or shaken by hand.
Castanets	Two small pieces of wood connected by string or elastic. The small pieces of wood are hit together with your hand and produce clicks. The castanets originated from Spain.
Tam Tam	The Tam Tam is also referred to as a gong. It is struck with a soft-headed mallet or beater.
Triangle	The triangle is a piece of metal bent into a triangle shape. To produce a sound it is held by a small loop of material at the top and struck with a metal beater.

Definite Pitch

Indefinite Pitch

Triangle

Tambourine

Xylophone

Timpani

VOICE TYPES

- Choral music is written for four main types of voice - Soprano, Alto, Tenor and Bass.

- This is often abbreviated to **SATB**.

- For Grade 5 Music Theory, as well as Soprano, Alto, Tenor and Bass you should also be aware of the Mezzo Soprano and Baritone.

- Below are these six voice types in order from highest to lowest:

Soprano - The soprano is the highest human voice. A soprano is usually a female voice. The usual voice range is from Middle C to approximately the second A above Middle C.

C   A

Mezzo Soprano - This voice range is slightly lower than a typical soprano and often goes from the A below middle C to the F or G at the top of the stave.

A   F

Alto - The Alto is usually the lowest voice range you will have for the female voice. The voice range is from the G below middle C to the highest D on the stave.

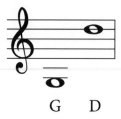

G   D

Tenor - The tenor voice is the highest in the ordinary male range. It sits between the Alto voice and Baritone voice. The usual range is from the C below middle C to the F just above middle C.

Baritone - The Baritone voice is usually a male voice type that lies between the Tenor and Bass. Its typical range is from two Gs below middle C to the E above middle C.

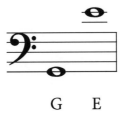

Bass - The Bass voice is the lowest of the voice types and is sung by the male voice. Its typical range is from the second F below middle C to the D just above middle C.

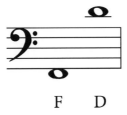

Key Fact

- The note ranges mentioned above are typical of each voice type. However, it is important to note that these ranges do vary between singers.

OPEN SCORE AND SHORT SCORE - WHAT'S THE DIFFERENCE?

- SATB music is written in one of two ways - **open score** or **short score**.

- **Open score** - an open score has four lines of music, with each voice having its own stave.

    - The soprano uses the treble clef.

    - The alto uses the treble clef

    - The tenor uses the treble clef with a little 8 at the bottom to indicate that they need to sing an octave lower than written

    - The bass uses the bass clef.

Open Score

- **Short score** - a short score has two lines of music.

    - The soprano and alto both use the treble clef stave.

    - The tenor and bass both use the the bass clef stave.

- On the short score it is easy for the singers to see which line of music is theirs by looking at which way the stem of the note is going. Take a look at the piece of music below to see this.

Short Score

ORNAMENTATION

- An ornament in a musical phrase is very much like a decoration on a Christmas tree. It is not essential to the flow of the music but it definitely makes the piece prettier and more exciting.

- An ornament is most often written in the music using a sign or symbol. However, they can also be written out, showing the specific notes you should play. Below we will show examples of each symbol and how it should be played.

- There are many different types of ornament – here are the most common ones you should be familiar with:

Upper Mordent

This is where we play the main note in the melody, quickly moving to the note above and then back down.

Lower Mordent

This is where we play the main note in the melody, quickly moving to the note below and then back up.

Trill

This is where we rapidly move between the main note and the note above. A trill can often end with a short closing pattern that uses the note below.

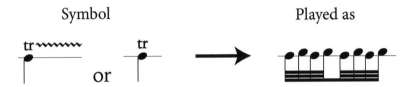

Appoggiatura

This is represented by a small note written next to the main note. It will take half the value of the note it is attached to and is often called a leaning note.

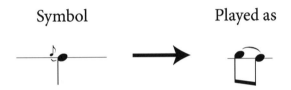

Acciaccatura

This is represented by a small note written next to the main note. Very much like an appoggiatura but this small note has a line through it. This note is often called a crushed note because it is literally crushed into the main note.

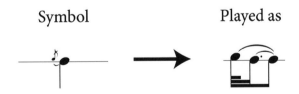

Turn

This is represented by a sideways letter S written above the note. It involves playing the main note, the note above the main note, the main note, the note below and then the main note again. This has to all be done very quickly.

Symbol   Played as

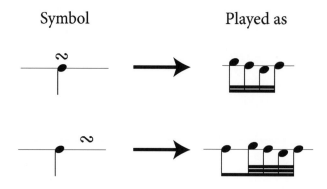

PERFORMANCE DIRECTIONS

- This is a list of words you should know for your Grade 5 theory. This list includes words and symbols from all grade (1-5).

- Within Grade 5 performance directions there are three different languages, Italian, French and German.

DYNAMICS

| | German |
| | French |

Term	Meaning
a niente	to nothing
crescendo, *cresc.*	gradually getting louder
decrescendo, *decresc., decres.*	gradually getting quieter
diminuendo, *dim., dimin.*	gradually getting quieter
fortissimo, *ff*	very loud
forte, *f*	loud
mezzo forte, *mf*	moderately loud
mezzo piano, *mp*	moderately quiet
piano, *p*	quiet
pianissimo, *pp*	very quiet
forte piano, *fp*	loud and then immediately soft
sforzando and sforzato, *sfz*	forced and accented
deciso	with determination
calando	getting softer, dying away (and slowing down)
mancando	fading away
morendo	dying away
perdendosi	dying away
sotto voce	in an undertone
estino	as soft as possible, lifeless
smorzando, *smorz.*	dying away in tone and speed

TEMPO

Term	Meaning
accelerando *accel.*	gradually getting quicker
adagietto	rather slow but faster than adagio
adagio	slow
affrettando	hurrying
alla breve	with a minim beat
alla marcia	in the style of a march
alla misura	in strict time
allargando	broadening (getting slower and louder)
allegretto	fairly quick
allegro	quick
andante	at a medium walking speed
andantino	slightly faster than andante
animando	becoming more lively
animato	animated
a piacere	at pleasure, the performer is not bound to follow exact rhythm
a tempo	in time, return to original speed
comodo	convenient
con brio	with vigour
con moto	with movement
doppio movimento	twice as fast
energico	energetic
flessibile	flexible, not in strict tempo
fretta	haste
furioso	furious, frenzied

Term	Meaning
grave	very slow and stately
incalzando	getting quicker
largamente	broadly
larghetto	rather slow
largo	slow and stately
lento	very slow, solemn
liberamente	freely
l'istesso tempo	at the same speed
lunga	long
lunga pausa	long pause
misura	measure (a bar)
moderato	moderately
mosso	with motion, animated
moto	movement, motion
movimento	movement, motion
precipitando	rushing, headlong
presto	fast
presto possibile	as fast as possible
rallentando, *rall.*	gradually getting slower
ritardando *rit.*	gradually getting slower
ritenuto	held back
tempo	speed, time
ritmico	rhythmically
rubato	with some freedom of time

Term	Meaning
senza misura	in free time
slargando	getting slower
slentando	getting slower
smorzando	dying away in tone and speed
stretto	quickening the speed
stringendo	gradually getting faster
tempo comodo	at a comfortable speed
tempo giusto	exact time
tosto	swift and rapid
veloce	swift
vivace	lively, quick
vivo	lively, quick
volante	flying, fast
bewegt	with movement, agitated
breit	broad, expansive
frei	free
gehend	at a steady speed
geschwind	quick
langsam	slow
lebhaft	lively
mässig	at a moderate speed
rasch	quick
rascher	quicker
schleppen	dragging
schleppend	dragging
schnell	fast
ziemlich	moderately

Term	Meaning
animé	animated and lively
cédez	yield, relax the speed
en animant	becoming more lively
en cédant	hurrying on
en mesure	in time
en pressant	hurrying on
en retenant	holding back
en serrant	becoming quicker
lent	slow
librement	freely
modéré	at a moderate speed
mouvement, *mouvt*	movement, motion
presser	hurry
ralentir	slow down
retenu	held back
serrer	hurry, quicken
serrez	hurry, quicken
vif	lively
vite	quick

MOOD AND EXPRESSION

Term	Meaning
affettuoso	tenderly
agitato	agitated
amabile	pleasant, amiable
amore	love
amoroso	loving
anima	soul, spirit
appassionato	with passion
brio	vigour, animation
calmato	calm, tranquil
cantabile	in a singing style
cantando	singing
capriccioso	in a whimsical, fanciful style
con anima	with feeling
con bravura	in a brilliant style
deciso	with determination
delicato	delicate
dolce	sweet, soft
dolente	sad, mournful
dolore	grief
doloroso	sorrowful
energico	energetic
espressione	expression
espressivo, *espress.* or *espr.*	expressive
felice	happy

Term	Meaning
feroce	fierce
fuoco	fire
furioso	furious, frenzied
giocoso	playful
giojoso	joyful, merry
grandioso	grandly
grazioso	graceful
impetuoso	impetuous
inquieto	restless
lacrimoso	sad
lamentoso	lamenting
leggiero	light, nimble
lontano	distant
lugubre	mournful
lusingando	coaxing, in a sweet style
maestoso	majestic
marziale	in a military style
mesto	sad
misterioso	mysterious
nobilmente	nobly
patetico	with deep feeling
piacevole	pleasant
piangevole	plaintive, lamenting
pietoso	tenderly

Term	Meaning
placido	calm, peaceful
rinforzando, *rf* or *rfz*	reinforcing
risoluto	bold, strong
scherzando	playful, joking
semplice	simple, plain
slancio	enthusiasm, impetus
solenne	solemn, grave
sospirando	sighing
spiritoso	spirited
strepitoso	noisy, boisterous
teneramente	tenderly
tenerezza	tenderness
tranquillo	calm
trionfale	triumphant
tristamente	sad, sorrowful
triste	sad, sorrowful
veloce	swift
vigoroso	vigorous, strong

Term	Meaning
Ausdruck	expression
ausdrucksvoll	expressively
bestimmt	with decision, definite
breit	broad and expansive
einfach	simple
Empfindung	emotion, feeling
feurig	fiery
fliessend	flowing
frisch	vigorous
fröhlich	cheerful, joyful
gesangvoll	in a singing style
innig	heartfelt, sincere
kräftig	with passion
Leid	grief, pain
Leidenschaft	passion
lieblich	lovely
lustig	cheerful
munter	lively
ruhig	peaceful
süss	sweet
traurig	sad
zart	tender, delicate

Term	Meaning
amour	love
animé	animated, lively
apaisé	calmed
calme	calm, tranquil
capricieux	in a whimsical, fanciful style
douce	sweet
emporté	fiery impetuous
flottant	floating
gracieux	graceful
joyeux	joyful
légèrement	light
lointain	distant
vif	lively

INSTRUCTIONAL WORDS

Term	Meaning
a due, a 2	for two performers or instruments
ad libitum, ad lib.	at choice, played freely
a piacere	at pleasure, performer is not bound to the exact rhythm given
attacca	go straight on to the next section of music
bis	twice, indicates the repetition of a short passage
coll' ottava	with the octave, indication to keyboard to double the note at the octave
colla parte	keep with the soloist, a direction to the accompanist
colla voce	keep with the singer, a direction to the accompanist
come prima	as before
come sopra	as above
con sordini, con sord.	use the mute
da capo, D.C.	repeat from the beginning
dal segno, D.S.	repeat from the sign
divisi, div.	divided, a direction to orchestral players to divide into groups
fine	the end
G.P.	an indication to players that everyone in the ensemble is to be silent
in relievo	prominent, make the melody stand out
l'istesso	the same
loco	at the normal pitch after having used an 8va direction
lunga pausa	long pause
muta	change - move from one instrument to another or change tuning
naturale, nat.	in the ordinary way
obbligato	obligatory, indicating instrument has an important role
pausa	a pause

Term	Meaning
prima volta	first time
repetizione	repetition
seconda volta	second time
segue	go straight on
sempre	always
senza sordini, senza sord.	without mute
simile, sim.	in the same way
sostenuto	sustained
sotto	below
sotto voce	in an undertone
tacet	silent
tutti	all, everyone
unisono	in unison
volti subito, V.S.	turn the page at once
gebunden	joined
vorgetragen	brought out, prominent
wieder	again
à deux, à 2	for two performers or instruments
en dehors	prominent, make the melody stand out
enlevez	take off, for a pedal or mute
fin	end

PERFORMANCE TECHNIQUES AND ARTICULATION

Term	Meaning
al tallone	use the bow at the heel
a punto d'arco	use the bow at the point
arco	use the bow
col legno	with the wood, play with the wood of the bow rather than the hair
con sordini	with mutes
flautato	flute-like, direction for natural harmonics on strings
glissando, gliss	a rapid scale
legato	smoothly
leggiero	light and nimble
mano destra, *m.d.*	right hand (piano)
mano sinistra, *m.s.*	left hand (piano)
marcato, *marc.*	emphatic, accented
martellato	strongly accented
muta	change from one instrument to another
naturale	in the ordinary way
parlando	speaking, sing in a conversational style
pesante	heavy
pizzicato, *pizz.*	direction for string players to pluck the strings rather than bowing
portamento	slide from one note to the next
saltando, saltato	springing, a lightly bouncing bow tehcnique on string instruments
secco	crisp (literally dry)
soave	gentle, smooth
sonoramente	resonant, with rich tone
sonoro	resonant tone
sordino	mute
sostenuto	sustained

Term	Meaning
spiccato	detached - a bouncing bow technique on string instruments
staccato	detached
sul G	only play on the G string
sul ponticello	play near the bridge
tremolando, tremolo, trem.	trembling, a direction for the rapid reiterations of a single note or alternations of different notes
tenuto	held
tre corda	release the left pedal (piano)
una corda	press the left pedal on the piano which makes the piano only play 'one string'
vibrato	vibrating
am Frosch	use the bow at the heel
an der Spitze	use the bow at the point
Dämpfer	mute
Flatterzunge, Flzg.	flutter tonguing - for wind instruments
gesangvoll	in a singing style
à la pointe	use the bow at the point
au talon	use the bow at the heel
détaché	detached, usually applied to string instruments
lourd	heavy
martelé	strongly accented
sautillé	springing, a lightly bouncing bow technique on string instruments
sec	crisp (literally dry)
sonore	resonant, with a rich tone
sourdine	mute

MISCELLANEOUS

Term	Meaning
a	at, to, by, for, in, in the style of
a cappella	unaccompanied (referring to choral music)
al	to the, in the manner of
alla	to the, in the manner of
alt	high
assai	very
ben	well
bene	well, very
bravura	skill, brilliance
brilliante	brilliant
col	with
come	as, similar to
comodo	convenient
con	with
corda	string
corde	strings
da	from
e	and
ed	and
eguale	equal
facile	easy
giusto	exact
licenza	licence, freedom
lunga	long

Term	Meaning
ma	but
mano	hand
meno	less
mezzo	half
mezza	half
misura	measure
molto	very, much
niente	nothing
non	not
nuovo	new
ossia	alternate, or
ostinato	persistent
ottava, *ott.*	octave
pedale	pedal
per	by, for, through, to
più	more
pochettino	a little
poch.	a little
pochissimno	very little
poco	a little
poi	then

Term	Meaning
ponticello	bridge on a string instrument
possibile	possible
prima	first
primo	first
quasi	resembling
rigoroso	strict
seconda	second
secondo	second
semplice	simple, plain
sempre	always
senza	without
sino	until, up to
sopra	above
sordino, sord.	mute
sotto	below
subito	suddenly
sul, sulla	on the
tanto	so much
tasto	the fingerboard of a string instrument
tre	three
troppo	too much
uno	one
unisono, unis.	in unison
voce	voice
volta	time

Term	Meaning
aber	but
als	than
doch	however, yet
ein	a, one
einfach	simple
etwas	somewhat, rather
immer	always
kräftig	strong
mit	with
nach und nach	gradually
nicht	not
noch	still, yet
ohne	without
schwach	weak
sehr	very
stark	strong
süss	sweet
und	and
viel	much
voll	full
wenig	little
wieder	again
zu	to, too

Term	Meaning
à	at, to, by, for, in, in the style of
assez	enough, sufficiently
avec	with
comme	as, similar to
égal	equal
et	and
fin	end
main	hand
mais	but
moins	less
non	not
pédale	pedal
peu	little
plus	more
sans	without
seul	alone
sourdine	mute
sous	under
très	very
un	one
voix	voice

SYMBOLS

𝄐	pause		diminuendo
staccato	staccato		crescendo
tenuto	tenuto		glissando
accent	accent	8va - - - -	octave higher
staccatissimo	staccatissimo		up bow
Ped.	press right pedal (sustain)		down bow
Ped. ✳ *Ped.*___	release pedal at the symbol or vertical line		tremolo
	arpeggiated, spread the chord	𝄋	segno
	tie		
	slur		
	repeat		
	coda		

FREE RESOURCES

Download resource sheets that match each chapter at

musictheoryfoundations.com/book/resources

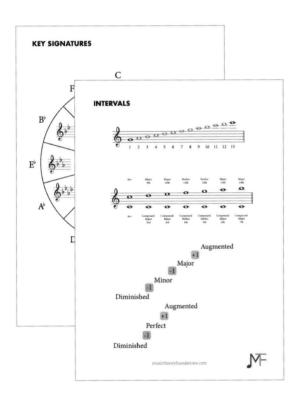

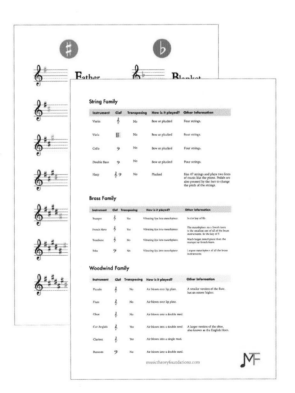

Printed in Great Britain
by Amazon

17998435R00069